MW01107136

SMALL BUSINESS GUERRILLA GUIDE TO SIX SIGMA

HOW TO SYSTEMATICALLY CUT COSTS AND BOOST PROFITS, EVEN IN TOUGH TIMES

BY

JAY ARTHUR

Upgrade Your KnowWare!

Published by LifeStar Publishing
2244 S. Olive St.
Denver, CO 80224
(888) 468-1537
lifestar@rmi.net
www.qimacros.com

ISBN 1-884180-26-4

Publisher's Cataloging-in-Publication Data
Arthur, Jay
    Small Business Guerrilla Guide to Six Sigma / by Jay Arthur
       p.   cm.
    Includes bibliographical references.
    ISBN 1-884180-26-4
    1. Business
    2. Quality

HF5549.5M63A47   2004
658.3'14–DC20   00-193560 CIP

Printed in the United States of America
10 9 8 7 6 5 4 3 2 1

CONTENTS

THE POWER OF SMALL BUSINESS

According to the SBA, small businesses:
- Represent 99.7% of all employers and 97% of exporters
- Create 75% of new jobs
- Employ 50.1% of the private sector work force
- Account for 39.1% of all high tech jobs
- Generate 40.9% of private sales

Yet according to recent studies, small businesses aren't leveraging one of the biggest trends in cost cutting and profit improvement available today: Six Sigma. Why not? Because they think it will cost too much, take too long, and provide questionable results.

Fortunately, small businesses can succeed at Six Sigma far more easily than big businesses, because small businesses are lighter on their feet, more flexible, and faster to adapt. When you simplify Six Sigma down to its essence, you can get big benefits with a minimal investment. But you have to ignore the prevailing wisdom about how to implement Six Sigma, because it's designed for Big Business, not small. To beat big business at their own game, you have to outsmart them. This book will show you how.

LEARNING TO **FISH**

The secret to Six Sigma is learning how to use performance measurements to FISH:

Focus: Laser-focus the improvement effort, because problems aren't spread all over your business, they are clustered in small areas that you can find and fix. There are hidden gold mines in your business, but you will need the tools of Six Sigma to find them!

Improve: Analyze the root causes and make improvements that will systematically cut costs and boost profits by $20 out of every $100 you spend.

Sustain: Monitor and maintain the new level of improvements, because otherwise you'll fall back into old methods and lower levels of performance.

Honor: Honor your progress. Recognize and reward improvements. Refocus and start on a new problem or issue.

BOOST PRODUCTIVITY AND PROFITS IN TOUGH TIMES

Ever noticed how some companies seem to thrive in economic downturns and blow past their competitors? Wouldn't you like to be one of them?

You can and here's why: neither your customers nor your suppliers control the greatest profit making opportunity in your business. You do.

There are hidden gold mines in your day-to-day business processes that you've been unable to tap using common sense, gut feel, and trial-and-error. The very techniques that allowed you to bootstrap your business and grow it to the current level will hit a wall and will stop working at about 3-sigma—a 1-2-3% error rate. This means that across your ordering, billing, purchasing, payments, and fulfillment processes your customers experience a 6-12-18% error rate—*an error rate that is devouring your profits.*

In a recession you can't market your way out. You can't sell your way out, because customers are tightening their purse strings. You can't innovate your way out, because customers want proven solutions, not new untried ones.

You can, however, systematically improve your mission-critical processes—eliminating defects, delay, and waste that translate into *immediate profits.* No waiting! And best of all, your processes are totally within your control—you don't have to rely on anyone else to change your results.

This means that you can fill your revenue dips with money that had been lost in operations. You can turn your employees attention to solving operational problems *forever.*

Then, when the economy turns around as it always does, you will not only have more money but be able to offer better prices than your competition and still make obscene profits.

Six Sigma is the key to unlocking the treasure trove of lost profits in your business. Six Sigma can pick up where trial-and-error, gut feel, and common sense leave off.

A Tale of Two Factories

Every company has two "factories:"
- one that creates and delivers your product or service
- and a hidden "Fix-it" factory that cleans up all of the mistakes and delays that occur in the main factory.

If you're a 3-Sigma company (and most companies are no better than 3-Sigma, because that's as far as you can get on good old common sense and trial-and-error improvement), then the Fix-it Factory is costing you $25-40 of every $100 you spend.

If you're a $1 million company, that's $250,000-$400,000. In a $10 million company, that's $2.5-$4 million that could be added back to your bottom line. If you're a $100 million company, that's $25-40 million. If you're a $1 billion company, that's $250-$400 million. Just think what saving a fraction of that waste could do for your productivity and profitability!

The End of Common Sense

We know that there are wave lengths of light that we cannot see with our eyes. And low pitched and high pitched sounds that only our dogs can hear. The same is true in business, there are levels of defects that we can't detect, or if we can notice them we have trouble making sense of them. This level is around 1-3% defects or 3 Sigma.

When I worked in the phone company, managers used to say "Well it's just common sense," but what I've learned is that common sense will only get you to a 3% defect rate. Most hospitals get to a 1% error rate on things like infection rates and medication errors, but that's where they reach the edges of human perception, *the end of common sense.*

When you reach the end of what you can do with one problem solving technology (e.g., common sense), you need to look to the next level: systematic problem solving and the tools of Six Sigma.

THE TOP 10 WAYS YOU KNOW YOU NEED SIX SIGMA

1. **Heroic efforts** are routinely required to prevent delivering a bad product or service. This invariably involves a culture of heroism. One company I worked with prided themselves on "doing the impossible everyday."

2. **Customer complaints.** For every customer who complains about your product, there are 16 more that won't tell you directly. Each of these tells eight other people about why they don't like your product or service. *Word of mouth can kill you!*

3. **Supplier complaints.** Do your suppliers complain about the irrational last minute demands you make and how long it takes to get paid? *Word of mouth can kill you!*

4. **Employee whining:** "I can't do my job because _____ doesn't do theirs. Employees want to do a good job. What's stopping them?

5. **Blaming people** for poor quality. 99% of the problem is in your process, not your people. Six Sigma focuses on process.

6. **Knee jerk fixes** that fail. Common sense and gut feel stop working at the 3-sigma level. That's when you need the "common science" of Six Sigma to take you to the next level.

7. **Margins are low, expenses are high, growth is stalled.** Defects and delay eat away at margins and inflate expenses.

8. **Failures in the field.** How big is your warranty or repair department? How many people does it take to handle your customer service and tech support calls?

9. **Too many inspectors** checking quality. You can't inspect quality into your product or service, but you can build it in.

10. **Absenteeism and turnover.** Employees hate doing a poor job for customers. They get angry when the internal system prevents them from doing a good job. How are your systems preventing your employees from doing a good job?

FIREFIGHTING VS FIRE PREVENTION

Many people worry about how much Six Sigma will cost. J. M. Juran suggests the following way of thinking about the so-called "costs of quality."

1. If you don't do anything to ensure a quality product, the cost of *failures* will be too high. They require either *rework* (e.g., getting a car fixed under warranty) or *waste* (e.g., food spoilage in a restaurant).

2. Many companies, in a knee-jerk reaction to these failures institute heroic *inspection* efforts and *Fix-it Factories* to catch defective products or services before they reach the customer. Again, this requires significant *rework* and *waste*. In the worst cases, half the people are involved in inspection and defect removal (e.g., 50% of software development costs are for testing).

3. Six Sigma companies, on the other hand, focus on *preventing* defects, errors, and mistakes. If you don't puts defects in, then you don't have to find or fix them. This frees everyone to focus on meeting the needs of customers instead of fixing their complaints.

Unfortunately, most companies prefer firefighting to fire prevention. They simply don't do enough process improvement to prevent the waste and rework costs associated with inspection and failure. Your goal should be to find the optimum balance between prevention, inspection, and failure. As you move toward Six Sigma, total costs will decline even more.

MANUFACTURING VS SERVICE

I can't tell you how many times I hear people say: "Six Sigma...isn't that just for manufacturing?" The short answer is: No, Six Sigma is good for ANY business—information, service, administrative, whatever.

Why? Because **every business suffers from the two key problems that Six Sigma can solve: defects and delay.**

If you look closely at American industry, more and more manufacturing jobs are moving offshore. More than half of the gross national product comes from information and service industries like Microsoft and McDonalds. But these industries are lagging behind manufacturing in the quest for quality.

That's why there's so much opportunity for the business that decides to use Six Sigma to breakthrough to new levels of productivity and profitability—no one else is doing it!

When I first started working with TQM in the phone company, many people said it wouldn't work because TQM works for manufacturing, not services. I've heard many people say the same thing about Six Sigma. Nothing could be further from the truth. This is just a convenient way for crafty employees to dodge learning the improvement strategies.

WHAT IS MANUFACTURING?

Those activities relating to the development and production of tangible products. Other terms used to describe these are "plant floor," "production," "a fab," and sometimes "engineering" and "product development." Driven by the marketplace, most manufacturing functions have had to embrace improvement methodologies and SPC just to survive.

WHAT ARE SERVICES?

According to Peter Pande, the answer is: Sales, finance, marketing, procurement, customer support, logistics, IT, or HR in any organization, from a steel company to a bank to a retail store. A few of the other words used to describe these activities include: transactional, commercial, nontechnical, support, and administration. These business functions have tried to hide from TQM and Six Sigma and many have been successful at flying under the "radar." But this is often where the big savings await.

At an abstract level there's no real difference between a service process and a manufacturing one. They both encounter delays, defects, and costs. One may produce purchase orders instead of computers, bills instead of brake liners, but they all take time, cost money, create defects, cause rework, and create waste. When we focus on finding the few key measures of defects, delay, and cost that are hampering profits and productivity, breakthrough improvements are easy.

In an IT department, we might focus on downtime or transaction delays. We might focus on manual rework of order errors or the costs of fixing billing errors. Even a great manufacturing company with IT problems can suffer tremendously from the service side of the business.

In a hospital, we might focus on medication errors. We might focus on admission, diagnosis, treatment, or discharge delays. We might focus on the costs of medical errors that result in longer hospital stays.

Every aspect of your business follows a process; it may be a highly refined process or an error-prone, ad hoc one. Regardless of whether it's service or manufacturing, there are always defects in the process steps, delays between steps, and increased costs involved in reworking or scrapping some work product.

So, if you're a good manufacturing company, but need to improve your ordering, fulfilling and billing, use Six Sigma to simplify and streamline your "service" components. If you're a good service company, find some key defects, delays, or costs in which to make breakthrough improvements that will differentiate you from all your competitors.

THE SMALL BUSINESS GUERRILLA

Are you a Small Business Guerrilla? Are you willing to ignore the prevailing, but incorrect "wisdom" about how to implement a systematic improvement methodology like Six Sigma? Are you willing to start making immediate improvements in productivity and profitability *using only a small fraction of your employees, time, and money*? Or would you rather spend a lot of time and money and then have to wait up to a year for bottom-line, profit-enhancing results?

THIS BOOK'S FOR YOU!

If you've been reading about Six Sigma at GE and other big companies and wondered how you can get the benefits without the expense, then this book is for you. A 2003 study by Quality Digest magazine confirmed what I've known for years: *a handful of tools and methods are delivering most of the benefit of Six Sigma.* Focused application of these tools will carry you from average to excellent (3-sigma to 5-sigma) in as little as 18-24 months, *while delivering staggering improvements in productivity and profits*.

DON'T LET THE NAME FOOL YOU

Six Sigma...even the name sounds complex doesn't it? But it doesn't have to be. This book will cover the bare-bones essence you need to know to start making breakthrough improvements. Like most things in life, 20% of the methods and tools will give you 80% of the benefit. These are the tools I use day in and day out with clients and in my business to make quantum leaps in performance. You can too.

GET IN CHEAP!

You can spend $15,000 or more training one Six Sigma Blackbelt, but the methods in this book will carry you from 3-to-5 sigma without spending all that time and cash. And I'll even show you where to download FREE software to automate your problem solving efforts and accelerate your success.

You can do it the hard way or the easy way. It's up to you!

IN GOD WE TRUST, ALL OTHERS MUST BRING DATA

The March 2003 issue of Quality Digest Magazine explored the results of their Six Sigma Survey. What did they discover?

1. Small companies aren't pursuing Six Sigma. Why not? It costs too much using the traditional Six Sigma approach. It can cost $250,000 to train a black belt and bring them up to speed.

2. Companies pursuing Six Sigma seem to abandon it after two or three years. Why? One reason might be that the average life-span of CEOs is only 2-3 years. When leadership changes, Six Sigma vanishes. Every company and consultant is still using the time-honored but flawed top-down, all-or-nothing strategy for implementation. Over 50 years of research into how companies and cultures adopt changes like Six Sigma suggests that "to accelerate adoption you will want to REDUCE the number of people involved." Fewer people, faster implementation!

3. Six Sigma is under performing the media hype
- Only 64% of respondents agreed that Six Sigma had significantly improved profitability.
- Only 50% agreed that Six Sigma had improved customer satisfaction.
- Only 43% agreed that Six Sigma had improved job satisfaction among employees.

OUCH! This means that current approaches to implementing Six Sigma are delivering a paltry 2-sigma performance (30% failure). No wonder we're looking at so many companies abandoning Six Sigma. The companies that are getting results are doing something different. What is it?

4. You don't need Black Belts to get results
■ 80% agreed that you should use whatever tools are necessary to get the job done. But, when asked which methods and tools yielded the greatest results, survey respondents answered:
■ 87% cause-effect analysis (line, pareto, fishbone)
■ 35% process mapping (flowcharts)

- 26% Lean manufacturing
- 25% Benchmarking
- 20% Statistical process control (SPC) and process management (flowcharts, control charts, and histograms).
- 21% ISO 9000 standards

STOP THE INSANITY

These findings reflect my own experience that you can move rapidly from 3-sigma to 5-sigma using only flowcharts, a few key problem solving tools (line chart, pareto chart, and root cause analysis), and SPC to sustain and monitor the improvements.

So, why do companies both big and small spend so much money training black belts in all of the exotic tools of Six Sigma when most of the bang-for-the-buck comes from just these few simple tools? Beats me! It must be a common management delusion that complexity delivers value.

So will Six Sigma go the way of TQM and the Dodo bird? Unless companies adopt the proven implementation methods and tools I've laid out in the Six Sigma Guerrilla Guide, I'm afraid Six Sigma will die. It's already on a respirator in the intensive care unit and the leading consultants in the field are still prescribing treatments that clearly do not work.

Someone once said that the definition of insanity is doing the same thing over and over again expecting the same result. But isn't that what most companies and consultants are doing with Six Sigma? Trying to implement it in the same old flawed fashion?

When will they wake up and do some root cause analysis on processes that clearly aren't working?

How much of our precious economy are we going to waste on this iteration of quality?

It's up to you. Which path will you choose?

DON'T REINVENT THE WHEEL, HIJACK THE BUS

Years ago, when I first got started with Total Quality Management (TQM) we used a top-down, CEO-driven, all-or-nothing approach to implementing TQM, just like companies are doing with Six Sigma. Following the guidance of our consultants, we started and trained hundreds of teams that met for one hour a week. Two years later only a handful of teams had successfully solved a key business problem. Most were mired in the early steps of the problem solving process.

So I decided to try something radical: I applied TQM (now known as Six Sigma) to TQM. I looked at:

- Each stuck team as a "defect."
- The "delays" built into process: the delays between training and application and the delays between team meetings.

I researched and found better methods for doing everything involved in implementation.

1. Using just-in-time (JIT) training, I was able to close the gap between learning and application.

2. Using one-day root cause teams, I was able to eliminate the delay between team meetings. Solutions that used to take months, now took only hours.

3. Using the power of "diffusion", I was able to weave the methods and tools of Six Sigma into the organization with a minimum involvement of key resources.

4. Using root cause analysis, I was able to streamline and simplify the process of focusing the improvement so that we only started teams that *could* succeed. You see, Six Sigma, like TQM before it, is a data-driven process. **If you don't have data about the problem, Six Sigma just won't work.** You don't have to have perfect data; there's no such thing, but you do have to have data that can narrow your focus. If not, you're lost.

By systematically applying Six Sigma to Six Sigma, I found ways to eliminate the failures and accelerate the delivery of results. That's what I call Six Sigma Simplified.

PEOPLE, PROCESS, AND TECHNOLOGY

Consider that there are only three pillars of increased productivity and profits: people, process, and technology.

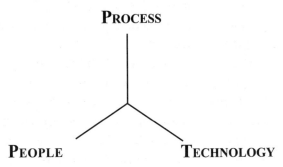

PROCESS

PEOPLE   TECHNOLOGY

Technology has been the holy grail of productivity in the last decade. So by all means buy the right technology, but if it's not the right solution to your problem, it may increase your costs without any bottom-line benefits. I developed the QI Macros for Excel (www.qimacros.com) to automate the creation of all of the graphs for Six Sigma because I needed a simple tool to work with my clients. It grew out of my own need for an inexpensive tool.

I was on a plane from Denver to Knoxville to teach a hospital about control charts when I opened up the in-flight magazine and found an interview with Larry Ellison, CEO of Oracle-the second-largest software company. The article tried to show that using its own software helped Oracle save $1 Billion dollars, but Ellison said something even more important: "The way you get quality is to define a set of processes and procedures and make sure they are implemented everywhere."

I was stunned! Here's a tech-CEO saying the key was consistent processes. And what he said next resonated with my two decades of software development and maintenance: "before we could automate anything, we had to standardize the new processes we would need. It meant simplifying and modernizing every procedure…"

"People ask the wrong question when they automate a company or process: Will this bunch of software allow us to [do] things the way we [do] them today?

The right question is: Will this allow us to do things the way we *should* do them for maximum effectiveness?"

After I graduated from the University of Arizona with a B.S. in Systems Engineering (the high art of optimizing systems), I got hired as a COBOL programmer for the phone company. There I started writing programs to automate existing manual processes that were so cumbersome and error prone that I often wondered what we hoped to gain by automating them. Here's what I learned: When you automate a poor process, you make it even more difficult and time-consuming to change. Things you might have changed on the fly now had to go through screening, prioritization, requirements, design, code, and test. Most changes took months, even years.

Years later, it seemed we were still doing the same things, but even dumber stuff. If an existing system caused too many errors, we'd write a mechanized system to fix the errors caused by the first system because the first one was deemed to complex to fix! There were systems that fixed addresses on outgoing bills (150,000/month were undeliverable). Why didn't we go back into the service order system and prevent the input of incorrect addresses? Because it might slow down our service reps. Silly huh?

So, if you want to maximize the benefit of your new information systems, use Ellison's and some of my advice:

1. Simplify and streamline your processes first.

2. Then choose or build a system that reflects the streamlined flow, not the old flow.

3. Expect each new system release to be error-prone. Use systematic problem solving to identify and remedy all of the requirements, design, and coding errors. Resolve problems at their source, not necessarily where they show up.

4. As your new system evolves, simplify and streamline the software to prevent the creeping complexity that will render it inflexible and unchangeable.

DISCIPLINE OF MARKET LEADERS

Several years ago, Michael Treacy and Fred Wiersema published an excellent book about market leaders. The Washington Post called it a common-sense map toward market leadership.

In the book, the authors argue that to successfully position yourself against your competition, you need to choose one of three paths: customer intimacy, operational excellence, or innovation. (Examples: Nordstroms, Wal-Mart, and Intel.)

OPERATIONAL
EXCELLENCE

CUSTOMER   INNOVATION
INTIMACY

The authors suggest that you choose one of these as the key goal to **maximize** so that customers will come to know you by your style. Even small-to-medium sized businesses can choose one of these strategies.

Customer intimacy evolved into CRM (Customer Relationship Management). And magazines like Fast Company argue the case for *innovation*.

Even if you don't choose *operational excellence* as your key strategy, you will want to ***optimize*** it in service of your main goal. Then, Six Sigma can help you reduce costs and increase speed and quality in ways that you've only dreamed possible.

I chose operational excellence for my business because I wanted to keep costs and prices low to reach as many businesses as possible. I optimize the use of technology (e.g., website, email) in service of this goal and as a means to deliver customer intimacy. Whichever focus you choose, Six Sigma will help you optimize your position in the marketplace.

THE PATTERNS OF GENIUS

As far as I can tell, there are only a few key patterns of genius in any business:

1. Creating new products and services (Innovation)
2. Marketing and sales (Relationships)
3. Delivering on your promises (Execution)
4. Systematic improvement of everything you do (Six Sigma)

SIX SIGMA IS THE SCIENCE OF SYSTEMATIC IMPROVEMENT

Six Sigma is a powerful set of methods and tools to eliminate defects and delay. It's not a panacea, but most day-to-day operational problems will yield to it. Most operational problems involve linear cause-effects that Six Sigma can fix.

Six Sigma won't directly fix morale (a complex, nonlinear problem), but it will help because employees will feel more engaged with the business.

Six Sigma won't directly fix your sales and growth problems, but it will influence your success over the long haul, because better products or services translate into customer loyalty.

Six Sigma won't solve your inability to innovate, but I have found that as you simplify and streamline your processes and products, marvelous insights reveal themselves. The science of complexity reveals that breakthroughs will then "emerge" from the chaos and complexity of your business. You don't have to "reengineer" a thing!

And, best of all, Six Sigma can fill the void when common sense, trial-and-error, and gut feel cease to deliver results.

Isn't it time you explored the patterns of genius in Six Sigma?

WHAT'S THE BIG IDEA?

Six Sigma is an aggressive, systematic method for break-through improvement in speed, quality and cost. Six Sigma focuses on bottom-line, profit-enhancing results, not training.

Most start-up companies have ad hoc processes with error rates of 15% (2.5 sigma). When the economy turns down, the costs of fixing defects can kill start-up companies like dot-coms.

Over time, most businesses get to error rates of around 3% (3 sigma or 30,000 defects per million) through **trial-and-error** and **common sense**. Because you can be profitable at this level, most companies fail to go any farther. But failure to "raise the bar" leaves you vulnerable to "quality" competitors.

What is Six Sigma Simplified? To go from 2 or 3 Sigma to 5 Sigma (233 PPM), you don't need exotic statistical tools, you only need **common science**: a few key tools and laser focus. With simple tools, most companies can easily and routinely find ways to save $250,000 and add it to the bottom line. For example, if it costs

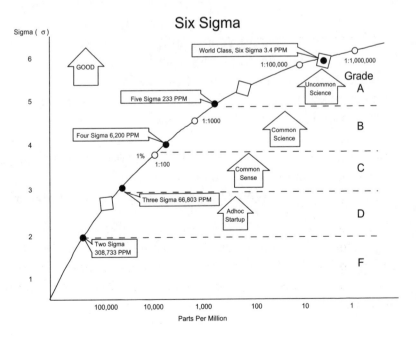

$10 to fix just one error, then going from 10,000PPM to 233PPM will prevent 9,777 errors and save $97,770. But there are additional costs of fixing an error–lost productivity (another $10), down-stream costs ($10-80), and lost sales. In reality, any defect or error can cost $50 or more when you add in all of the related costs.

MAKE IT HURT

Instead of measuring error rates in percentages (%), Six Sigma measures them in parts per million (PPM). The 1999 study of healthcare found that 1% of people admitted to a hospital *die* from medical mistakes, making healthcare the 8th leading cause of death. A 1% death rate is 10,000 deaths per million admissions.

Sigma (σ)	Defects/Million
1	690,000
2	308,733
3	66,803
3.5 Average	
4	6,210
5	233
6	3.4

In *Built To Last*, (Collins 1997), the authors mention the need for a BHAG or Big Hairy Audacious Goal. Using Six Sigma as a guide, you can measure your current performance in defects per million and set a BHAG of reaching the next level sigma.

So, if your computer system has 2% downtime, that's 20,000 minutes per million or about 3.5 sigma. Set a goal to reach 5 sigma (233 minutes/million).

WHY SIX SIGMA? WHY NOW?

In the late 90's, Jack Welch at GE applied Six Sigma to improving GE's performance. And Six Sigma is saving GE *BILLIONS of Dollars!* Without the widespread coverage of GE's success with Six Sigma, I doubt that it would be getting much attention.

CHANGE THE NAMES TO PROFIT THE CONSULTANTS

Over the years, I've had a chance to learn and study just about every "brand name" systematic improvement methodology. Guess what...*they are all pretty much the same.* To appear different, consultants have changed:
- the name to Six Sigma (from TQM)
- the acronyms to confuse the unwary (PDCA to DMAIC)
- the number of tools required for success
- the number of steps in the process (5 to 14 steps)

but...
- **the key tools are the same**

- **the process for using the tools is the same**

- **and the results are identical** assuming you can figure out how to use the wide range of tools and processes.

For these minor, cosmetic differences companies often charge $100,000 or more in *licensing* fees just to use their "methodology." Then you spend weeks in training just to get started. Is it any wonder that only big companies with deep pockets attempt to use these monolithic methods?

HOW IS SIX SIGMA DIFFERENT FROM TQM?

It's not. The underlying tools and processes are the same. They changed the acronyms to confuse the unwary: PDCA became DMAIC; QFD and DOE got grouped under DFSS (Design for Six Sigma). So, if you know TQM, you can quickly bridge that knowledge to Six Sigma.

If you don't know TQM, that's good; you have less to unlearn!

HOW IS SIX SIGMA IDEALLY DIFFERENT FROM TQM?

Ideally, the focus should shift from
- teams and training to *profits and productivity*;
- incremental improvement to *breakthrough improvement with bottom-line benefits*.

If you look closely at all of the articles about Six Sigma and it's implementation, you'll see that the approach to Six Sigma isn't any different from TQM. And over 50% of TQM efforts failed!

HOW IS SIX SIGMA SIMPLIFIED DIFFERENT?

Our Six Sigma Simplified "generic" methodology, as one customer put it: *"is a non-intimidating approach to systematic improvement that retains all of the goodness of Six Sigma without watering it down. "* Six Sigma Simplified is identical to the "brand names" with a few key exceptions:

1. You get the essential tools necessary to achieve the desired result, not a bunch of tools that are only used in rare cases.

2. You get the most streamlined, elegant process I have ever found for breakthrough improvement, without all of the extra steps.

3. You get the fastest, just-in-time training method that I've found anywhere for developing skill *and* delivering results in a matter of days, not weeks or months.

4. You get an easy-to-use, software tool kit to automate all of your Six Sigma activities. Our QI Macros for Excel software was designed to integrate with any Six Sigma System.

5. You save a small fortune in training and licensing fees, because there are none.

DON'T CONFUSE THE MEANS WITH THE ENDS

Too many companies are losing sight of the objective when it comes to Six Sigma. The goal is to cut costs, boost profits, and accelerate productivity; it's not the wholesale implementation of the Six Sigma methodology.

Want to know the biggest mistake big companies make implementing Six Sigma? They're trying to do it *everywhere*. Big business is saddled by the need to do things in a BIG way with lots of people, fanfare, and hype.

As a small business, you can't afford this kind of stupidity.

At the American Society for Quality's annual conference, many people stopped by our booth drawn by the promise of Six Sigma *Simplified*. They'd been buried in an avalanche of conventional wisdom that you have to make a major commitment to Six Sigma, spend lots of money training black belts, and wait years for results. Every one of these disheartened small business owners voiced the same questions: "Isn't there a better way?"

Of course there is, because all of the conventional wisdom and hype about Six Sigma is DEAD WRONG!

THE GOAL IS BOTTOM LINE, PROFIT-ENHANCING, PRODUCTIVITY BOOSTING RESULTS.

Six Sigma is merely a means to that end. Nothing more. It is not the one-size-fits-all, universal cure to what ails your business. Six Sigma is a power toolkit for solving two key business problems:

- **defects**—errors, mistakes, scratches, imperfections
- **delay**—when the customer's order is idle

You can't use it on morale. It won't help you design a successful marketing campaign. One portion called Design for Six Sigma (DFSS) will help you design more innovative products and bring them to market sooner, but it won't help you come up with the spark of brilliance that usually marks innovation.

RIGHT IDEA, WRONG LEADERS

If you've been reading anything about Six Sigma, you've heard it repeated endlessly that you want to get top leadership commitment to Six Sigma.

Back in the 1990s, I worked in the phone company when our CEO "committed" to quality. Hundreds of millions of dollars and almost five years later, the company abandoned TQM. Having the CEO on your side may help, but it's not the holy grail of gaining organization-wide commitment to Six Sigma.

The emerging science of networks suggests that it's *never* the formal, or hierarchical leadership that determines the success or failure of a culture change...it's the *informal* leaders—the hubs—in any "network" that determine success.

Formal Network

Informal Network

In *The Tipping Point*, Malcolm Gladwell argues that any idea (e.g., Six Sigma) "tips" into the mainstream when sponsored by one of three informal leaders: connectors, mavens, and salespeople.

Connectors connect people with other people they know. Think about your own company. Who is the center of influence that knows everybody and introduces everyone to everyone else?

Mavens connect people with technology. Who is the center of influence in your company who gets everyone on board with all the new changes in technology (e.g., Six Sigma, SPC, etc.).

Connectors and Mavens are what Seth Godin, author of *Ideavirus*, calls the *powerful sneezers*—someone who spreads an ideavirus. If you want to harness connectors and mavens to Six Sigma, you have to give them elite status—the inside track on the new methodologies.

Salespeople are what Seth would call a "promiscuous sneezer." They do it for money. When you follow the CEO-commitment rule, these folks will show up like vultures to a carcass. Beware.

THE CORPORATE IMMUNE SYSTEM

Let's not forget that every organization has laggards that are every bit as connected as the connectors, mavens, and salespeople. I call these people the *corporate immune system* because they fight infectious ideas with a zealotry that's unparalleled. How can you keep the laggards in the dark about the changes underway until it's too late? (Hint: Start small and crawl-walk-run your way to success by focusing on only the 4% of your business that causes over 50% of the waste, rework, and lost profit.)

Similarly, if you want to alienate the powerful sneezers and turn them into part of the immune system, don't let them in on the initial projects. Keep them out of the loop. They'll hate you for it.

Everett Rogers, in the book *The Diffusion of Innovations*, sites overwhelming research showing that the fastest ways to start a change are either autocratic (i.e., formal leadership) or word of mouth (i.e., informal leadership). In my experience, CEOs come and go (average tenure of a CEO is less than three years), but informal leaders are around forever.

So, everything you've heard about getting leadership committed to Six Sigma is essentially right, but they just had the wrong leadership. Get the informal leaders involved early and make them successful. They will sneeze the idea to everyone else in the organization. Once the initial 4% adopt Six Sigma, it will stick. After 16-20% adopt, it will become unstoppable.

If you want Six Sigma to succeed, you want to involve the sneezers in your organization and make them successful right from the start.

The small business guerrilla can reap the benefits of Six Sigma without incurring all of the costs just by using some unconventional wisdom backed by the decades of research into how to do it right the first time. Even if you don't fully commit to Six Sigma you can still get big, bottom-line benefits. And isn't that want you want anyway?

ALL-OR-NOTHING VS CRAWL-WALK-RUN

Traditional Six Sigma wisdom says that you have to take an all-or-nothing approach to Six Sigma. This too is dead wrong. It's a myth spread by Six Sigma consultants (promiscuous sneezers) who directly benefit from it.

The Six Sigma world seems to be increasingly divided between the haves and the have nots, the Six Sigma snobs and the plebian masses. The reigning wisdom seems to be that to succeed at Six Sigma, you have to embark on a total cultural transformation.

Sadly, I haven't heard anyone talking about the benefits they have achieved from implementing such a transformation. There seems to be this illusion that if you embark on Six Sigma, you'll magically be transported to a place of productivity and profitability. Nothing can be further from the truth. I've heard too many stories of massive investment in Six Sigma with little return. One quality auditor expressed concern that if we aren't measuring the ROI of Six Sigma; we're just fooling ourselves. After you pony up an estimated $250,000 (training, salary, projects, etc.) to develop a Black Belt, are you going to get at least $50,000 a project?

So why are all of these big companies trying to do it the all-or-nothing way? Because you can't be criticized for aggressively doing everything possible to implement Six Sigma (even though research says you should be punished for wasting so much money.)

THERE HAS TO BE A BETTER WAY

There is a better way that produces better results with minimal risk: the crawl-walk-run strategy. First, use the power of "diffusion" to implement Six Sigma: *start small* with the first 4% of your business, then the next 4%, and so on until you reach a critical mass where Six Sigma will sweep through the company, pulled forward by word of mouth. When I explain this "crawl-walk-run" approach to business owners, each one seems to awaken from his or her fog of despair and envision a path to Six Sigma that is doable.

SHOW ME THE MONEY

Because everyone wants to be certified as a black belt to enrich their resume and fatten their own bottom line, the black belt certification business is kicking into high gear. In every college town, someone is designing a certification program to crank out black belts like Detroit cranks out cars. In a couple of years, everyone will have a certification. Black Belts will be as common as high school diplomas. But it's not how much you know, it's what you can do with what you know.

One quality engineer expressed concern that with all of our manufacturing going offshore to places where workers are cheap, there won't be enough work in this country for the existing quality workers. To this I say: we haven't begun to work on the quality of our service and information businesses. No matter what business you're in, there will always be a demand to be better, faster, and cheaper than your competition, and that's the heart of Six Sigma-quality, speed, and profitability.

BE A MONEY BELT!

The corporate jury is still out on Six Sigma. Without dramatic examples of success, Six Sigma will go the way of TQM and quality circles. I encourage you to be a Six Sigma Money Belt™. Show me the money! Develop a rich resume of successful projects that give meaning to your skills. Tell your leadership, your customers, and the world how much you've saved.

Otherwise, Six Sigma will die out like its predecessors. Then by 2010 a new buzzword will give life to the same improvement methods. And we'll start a new round of corporate cultural transformation and training. By then I might be jaded enough to start my own certification program and be satisfied with training unsuspecting converts in the exotic depths of statistics without regard for their success on the job.

No, probably not.

TURN YOUR CASH COW INTO A GOLDEN GOOSE

I spent 21 years working in various parts of the Bell System—one of the best cash cows of the last century. Since profits were dictated by the public utilities commission, there was no need to get too good. Managers and employees could get by on trial-and-error to reveal common sense ways to improve the business. After divestiture in 1984, however, this changed. In 1990, the Baby Bell I worked for started to try TQM–Total Quality Management. Frustrated by the glacial slowness of teams and the paltry returns, I started to look for ways to use TQM to drive breakthrough improvements. In 1994-1995 I lead teams that, in a matter of months, saved $20 million in postage expense and $16 million in adjustment costs. One of my colleagues lead teams that reduced computer system downtime by 74% in just six months. Unfortunately, just as we started to get the knack for making breakthrough improvements, the leadership team switched fads, jumped on the reengineering bandwagon, and downsized the TQM department. Since then, I've helped other companies find ways to save $250,000/project or more. And you can to, using the power of Six Sigma.

Has your business grown into a cash cow? Are you comfortable with your current level of productivity and profitability? Or do you still have a nagging feeling that they could be significantly higher? Well they can be and here's why:

I have found that virtually all companies grow from wobbly start-ups into a cash cows using trial-and-error and common sense, but then most companies simply stop improving. They reach the limit of what's possible using common sense alone. Most companies stop improving when they reach 1%, 2%, or 3% error levels in marketing, sales, ordering, fulfilling, and billing. And each of these errors costs far more to fix than it did to create.

The very thing that took you to sustainable profitability will take you no farther. To turn your Cash Cow into a Golden Goose you will need the common science of Six Sigma to rise to 5-Sigma (less than 300 PPM).

HERE'S WHAT YOU CAN ACCOMPLISH WITH SIX SIGMA:

1. **Double your speed.** Most companies have extensive delays *built into* their processes. It usually takes no more than two days to flowchart a process and identify how to eliminate the delays, slashing your cycle time by 50% or more.

2. **Double your quality** by reducing defects in your main factory by 50% or more. Properly focused, teams can do this in one day or less.

3. **Increase your profits** by slashing the cost and delays associated with the Fix-It Factory. Every dollar you used to spend on fixing problems can now be refocused on growing the business or passed right through to the bottom line.

WHAT CUSTOMER'S WANT

Customers only want three things. They want you to be:

- **better** than your competition (fewer defects, fewer failures)
- **faster** than your competition (time to respond to request)
- **cheaper** than your competition (more total value)

To begin to understand your customer's needs and improve your ability to meet them, you will want to develop a way to measure them *over time*–by hour, day, week, or month.

Measures are like a respiration or heart rate monitor in a hospital; they let you know how your business is doing. Measures track how well your product or service meets the customer's requirements. Strategically positioned at critical hand off points in the process, they provide an early warning system. For each key customer requirement there should be one or more measures that monitor and predict whether you will deliver what they require.

Requirement	Measurement	Period
Better	Number of defects	hour
	Percent defective	day
Faster	commitments missed	week
	time in minutes, hours, days	month
Cheaper	cost per unit	shift
	cost of waste or rework	batch

There are usually only a few key customer requirements for any product or service. Identify your customer's requirements for your product or service. What do they want in terms of better, faster, and cheaper. Then, based on your customer's needs, identify how you can measure it with defects, time, or cost. Finally, identify how often you will measure: by minute, hour, day, week, or month.

Example: An independent muffler shop found that customers wanted a *commitment* about when they could pick up their car (no waiting). He measured installation time by model and age to develop accurate commitments.

USE THE 4-50 RULE

Even though every manager has heard the 80-20 rule, they still try to use Six Sigma everywhere. But Six Sigma is like peanut butter—the wider you spread it, the thinner it gets. Remember that if you try to use Six Sigma everywhere, 80% of your effort will only produce 20% of the benefit.

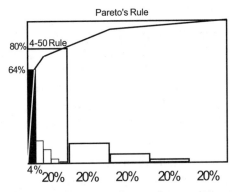

What if you could get over half of the "benefit" from Six Sigma by investing in just 4% of the business? You can! Pareto's 80/20 rule is a power law. Power laws aren't linear, they grow by an order of magnitude. So, if you believe in Pareto's rule, you have to believe that it applies within the 20%: 4% of the business will cause 64% of the waste and rework. Wherever I go, I find that four percent of transactions cause over 50% of the rework. Four percent of Americans have over half the wealth. And so on.

Better still: The research into the diffusion of innovation shows that transformational change begins with less than five percent of the work force (4%). It also suggests that **to accelerate the implementation of Six Sigma you will want to reduce the number of people involved**.

Rather than waste most of your hard-earned dollars on a widespread implementation, focus and achieve results in just a few key areas. Then like seeds in the wind, word of mouth will spread the change to a few neighbors, and before long, virtually the entire company will have converted with minimal resistance and expense.

SET BHAGS

Conventional wisdom suggests that the goal is incremental improvement. But if 4% of the business can produce over half the lost productivity and lost profit, why aren't you shooting for what Jim Collins, (*Built to Last* and *Good to Great*) calls a Big Hairy Audacious Goal (BHAG).

Service Example: One computer operations VP set a goal of a 50% reduction in on-line system downtime for the year. Even though no one thought it possible, the group reduced downtime by 74% in just six months using Six Sigma Simplified.

IT Example: One information systems VP set a goal to cut order errors in half over the year. The IT group reduced order errors from 17% to 3% in just four months using Six Sigma Simplified, an 82% improvement.

Set a BHAG to reduce defects in one of your mission critical systems by 50% in six months:

- Order errors
- Product or service defects
- Billing errors
- Purchase order errors
- Payment errors

Set a BHAG to reduce cycle time in a customer critical process by 50% in the next six months. You'll be surprised how far such a goal will take you.

Or, using Six Sigma as a guide, set the next level Sigma as a target. If you're at 3-Sigma, go for 4-Sigma, and so on. Your target for world-class quality is at least 5-Sigma (233 defects per million). And you can get there in 18-24 months using Six Sigma Simplified. If GE can save $2 Billion in one year by focusing on Six Sigma, how much could you save?

USE SWAT TEAMS OF EXPERTS

The old quality circle concept relied on volunteer teams that met once a week *forever*.

Six Sigma Simplified demands SWAT teams of subject matter experts that meet briefly (a day or two) and then disband. Once you've laser-focused the problem to be solved, it's easy to figure out who should be involved in the root cause analysis.

Then, following the Six Sigma Simplified methodology, the experts can usually find the root cause in one day or less. Once root causes are identified the team can disband and leadership can oversee the implementation of the proposed solutions and track the results.

You Can't Learn To Swim, Without Getting Wet

Conventional wisdom suggests that you need to train at least one blackbelt. This means that you have to send one of your top people away for four weeks at a cost of $15,000 or more to get trained in all of the "just-in-case" tools and techniques of Six Sigma. This, of course, is another myth propagated by Six Sigma consultants that want you to spend money on training.

Sadly, many employees want the blackbelt training, not so that they can help the company, but so that they can fatten their resume and get a better job somewhere else. Bye bye investment!

I just got a request for proposal from a hospital to train their leaders and staff members. They wanted at least 20 staffers recognized as green belts and 20 recognized as black belts.

Big contract, lots of training. Sounds seductive, doesn't it?

Well, all that training is great for the trainer's pocketbook, but bad for customers. You end up with highly trained, accredited, but inexperienced improvement leaders. This lack of experience can kill Six Sigma. I suggested that what they really want are experienced professionals that can diagnose, treat, and heal issues concerning speed, quality of care, and costs.

The sad truth is that you lose 90% of what you learn in a classroom if you don't use it within 48-72 hours. And isn't that what happens: you go to training and come back after a week to a pile of work. By the time you're caught up, you can't remember what you learned just a few days ago.

Looking at this from a Six Sigma perspective, the delay between training and application isn't just about the waste of time, but also about loss of skill. The only way to reengineer this problem is to eliminate the delay: **just-in-time training.**

In the early 1990s, when I was lured into the in-depth training paradigm, I'd spend a week using a Deming Prize Winning methodology to train 20 team leaders. They, in turn, would start teams that met once a week for an hour. Months went by. Years went by. Nothing got better.

You can't learn to swim without getting wet.

So, unbeknownst to my company leadership, I changed the process. I shortened the training down to a couple of hours. I would only teach it immediately prior to solving a real problem. Then, in a day or two, I'd guide the team to a solution. They got experience and the good feelings associated with success. Surprisingly, many of these team members could then apply the same tools and process to other problems with equal success. I discovered that I was creating highly skilled, but essentially untrained team leaders in a matter of one day. To strengthen their abilities, I'd occasionally conduct a one-day intensive to review what they'd learned through experience. This helped reinforce what they knew and fill in any gaps.

With one day of experience and a day of review training, I was accomplishing what the old-style week of training and endless meetings could not. And, we were getting bottom-line benefits simultaneously.

Sadly enough, by the time I figured this out, the Quality Department was on its last legs because it had failed to do more than waste time and money defining and measuring cumbersome, error-prone processes that needed major repair. A year later, the department was disbanded and the people laid off.

Don't let this happen to you. Consider using just-in-time training to prep your teams for immediate immersion in problem solving or SPC. Use real data. Use real problems. From the time we are born, we learn by watching other people do things. When you guide a team through the process, they learn an enormous amount just by watching you. Then reinforce what they've learned unconsciously with one-day review training.

You'll save your company time and money, get immediate results, encourage the adoption of Six Sigma by satisfied employees, generate good buzz, and have more fun.

Lesson plans for just-in-time training are included in the Six Sigma Simplified Instructor Guide (qimacros.com/instructor.html).

Make your training stick!

BARRIERS TO SIX SIGMA

Sadly, the biggest barriers to Six Sigma are human and psychological, not methods or technology. People often find it's easier to fight a new idea than to implement it! Most of this resistance is about fear of one kind or another. Here's the barriers I've encountered and some ways to handle them.

1. PEOPLE DON'T LIKE BEING MEASURED.

Why? Fear! Let's face it, most companies use measurement to blame and punish people, not improve processes. Is it any wonder that employees and managers resist measurement? Crafty dodgers use artful, distracting challenges to delay, derail, or ditch measurements. Here are some of the responses I've developed:

- Challenge the statistics or the statistician. One doctor challenged a hospital QA manager with: "Where did you get these formulas [for control charts]? Where does the standard deviation come from?"

  Redirect: You must already know the answer, so why don't you share it with us?

  Snappy answer: "That's like asking: 'Why are there 60 minutes in an hour?' These are widely accepted statistical techniques. If you're really interested in the details, I'll get you a book to read."

- Challenge the data. I can't tell you how many times I've heard: "That's not the 'right' data." Or "That data's not accurate or valid."

  Teach them: Let's face it, no data is perfect. There's measurement error caused by measurement methods and instruments. And, because people fear being punished for poor performance, defects are systematically and routinely underreported by a factor of at least two.

  Snappy answer: "You must have better data. Show it to us." If they don't have better data, tell them to get over it and use what they've got. Or kick them off the team.

■ Challenge the focus. "We have more important problems than this!"

Snappy answer: "How do you know there are more important problems? Where's your data? Show it to us." If they don't have a line graph, pareto charts and cost of quality analysis to prove that their problem is more important, ask them to participate in this problem or drop out.

2. MACHO MAN

Most managers, directors, and VPs don't want to believe that they are wasting 20-40% of their budget. If there were such hidden stashes of $250,000 or more, shouldn't they have found it by now? After all, gut feel, common sense and trial-and-error has served them well in the past. And what does it say about them if they can't find it? (They fear looking stupid or inept. Also remember that numbers are systematically distorted to make everyone look better. Six Sigma is going to adjust the counting methods, but rarely in a positive direction.)

Reframe: It's not that what you're doing hasn't taken you a long way, it's just that gut feel and common sense stop working at around 3-4 sigma. They just won't take you any farther.

Metaphor: In the 1800s doctors believed that sickness was caused by an ill wind or bad blood. But, with the development of the microscope, Pasteur was able to "see" the invisible agents of disease. The tools of Six Sigma, like Pasteur's microscope, enable us to see the seemingly invisible root causes of waste and rework.

3. ACHIEVERS VS PROBLEM SOLVERS

Businesses have employees with two opposing points of view: Achievers who want to set and achieve goals, and Problem Solvers who want to fix broken processes. Six Sigma sounds like ambrosia to the Problem Solvers and more like dog droppings to the Achievers.

Reframe: Six Sigma will free up resources to achieve more of what you want to accomplish.

4. BIG PICTURE VS DETAIL

Half of your employees are "blue sky" thinkers. They love the big picture but hate the detail. Six Sigma is a rigorous, detail-oriented process. Your detail thinkers will dive in without good direction available from the big picture thinkers, and the big picture thinkers will resist taking the mission-critical issues down to an actionable level.

Reframe: Haven't you waited long enough to dig down to the root cause, or do you just want to keep watching from a distance as the business drowns in its own waste and rework?

5. EVOLUTIONARIES VS REVOLUTIONARIES

Evolutionaries want to improve the business. They make up about 65% of the workforce. Revolutionaries want to reengineer the business. They want to make a difference. Paradoxically, businesses need both styles to succeed.

Reframe: We need to create new products *and* improve our methods of delivering them to keep the competition at bay.

6. HERO WORSHIP

Companies rarely let defective products escape their walls; usually by brute-force heroics of a small band of self-sacrificing perfectionists who are routinely rewarded for their heroics. Preventing problems would steal their claim to fame.

Reframe: It's not that what you're doing hasn't taken you a long way, it's just that the secret to success lies in consistency and repeatability, not random acts of heroism.

7. FIX-IT FIEFDOMS

Most companies have groups of people who do nothing but fix mistakes created elsewhere in the business. The managers and employees in these groups have based their whole careers on finding and fixing errors in the product or service. And they'll fight anything that will eliminate their jobs (fear).

Reframe: Don't you get tired of fixing the same old errors every day? You're the expert on the most common types of errors.

Wouldn't you rather help fix the processes that create them? (Shift their focus from fixing products to fixing processes.)

8. INSTINCTS VS INSTRUMENTS

In almost every team I facilitate, I have one or two people who think they "know the answer." They've got a pet theory which is invariably destroyed during the root cause analysis.

Metaphor: Most barnstormers like to fly by the "seat of their pants," but combat pilots know that your instincts can get you killed. They know that when you're flying blind you have to trust your instruments, not your instincts.

Reframe: Instincts are ideal for making decisions based on insufficient data, but they are rarely sufficient when you have data to analyze.

9. FEAR OF LOOKING STUPID

I don't know what it is about school and grades, but most of us are afraid of looking or feeling stupid. And most people are still afraid of the math behind Six Sigma.

Reframe: We've got computers to handle the math; we just want you to understand how to use the graphs to optimize performance and profitability. And we've hired experts to show you how.

Of course there are many more human issues than these, but these are some of the most common ones I've run across. Which ones have you found? How have you handled them?

SIX SIGMA PROCESSES

There are *four key processes* in Six Sigma:

LASER FOCUS

Purpose: To focus the effort in ways that will achieve breakthrough improvements in speed, quality, and cost. Using the voice of the customer, business and employee, you develop a "Master QI Story" that links and aligns multiple teams and improvement efforts to achieve quantum leaps in performance improvement.

IMPROVE SPEED, QUALITY, COST

Purpose: To improve customer satisfaction by identifying and eliminating the root causes of problems involving time, defects, or cost. This process uses data to analyze problems and eliminate their root causes. With laser-focus you can fix the 4% of your business that generates over 50% of the waste and rework.

SUSTAIN THE IMPROVEMENT

Purpose: To define and stabilize any process. Also known as SPC-statistical process control, this process uses data to evaluate the ability of any business process to *predictably* and *consistently* meet the customer's requirements. It serves as a basis to systematically improve any process and maintain the gains from your improvements.

HONOR YOUR PROGRESS

Purpose: To recognize, review, and refocus.

Step	Activity	Tools
1	**Focus** with laser-like precision	Tree Diagram Line Graph Pareto Chart
2	**Improve** delay, defects, and costs	Fishbone
3	**Sustain** the improvement	Control Charts
4	**Honor** your progress	

YOUR "MILLION DOLLAR MONEY BELT" IMPROVEMENT STRATEGY

1. Create a Master Improvement Story

2. Track Key Indicators

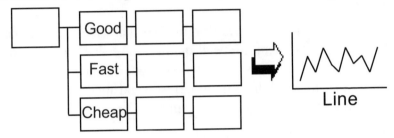

3. Define the Problem

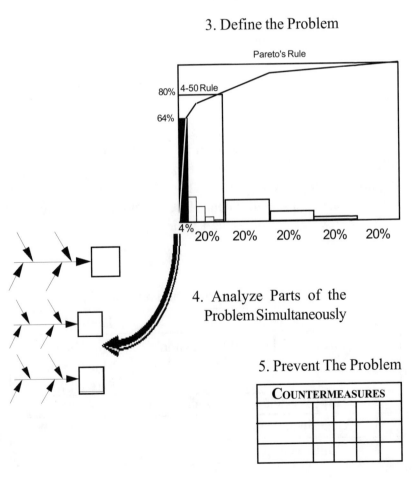

4. Analyze Parts of the Problem Simultaneously

5. Prevent The Problem

COUNTERMEASURES				

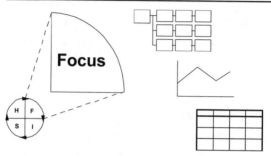

Laser Focus

Purpose: Focus the improvement effort to avoid wasting valuable time and money.

Key Tools
- Tree diagram
- Line graph
- Pareto chart

Process

FISH	Step	Activity
Focus	1	Use the Voice of the Customer to develop a Master Improvement Story.
	2	Identify and track the indicators
	3	Set targets for improvement.
Improve	4	Initiate process improvements
Sustain	5	Sustain the improvements
Honor	6	Honor your progress
	7	Review and refocus objectives, teams, and improvement efforts as required.

Focus, Focus, Focus.

The first step in focusing your improvement efforts is to create a balanced scorecard and a master improvement story. The master improvement story identifies your key areas for improvement, measurements, targets, and effects of those improvements. The best tool for doing this is the tree diagram.

This tool can easily demonstrate the "balanced scorecard" approach that focuses on four key areas: financial growth, customer satisfaction, learning and growth, and quality. Financial growth and customer satisfaction are effects of providing better quality products faster at a lower cost and higher perceived value. Learning and growth focus on employee skill development and the availability of information systems to support learning. Quality focuses on using Six Sigma to create breakthrough improvements in cycle time, defects, and cost.

BHAG: Once you've identified your key measurements for each of these goals, set a Big Hairy Audacious Goal (BHAG) for improvement. Forget the 10% improvement. Go for 50% reductions in cycle time, defects, costs, system downtime and so on. Go for 50% improvements in financial results and customer satisfaction. I have found that when you go for 10% improvements, you only get 10% ideas. When you go for 50% improvements, you get 50% or bigger ideas, and you often get 70-80% improvements. Breakthroughs! BHAGs also force you to narrow your focus to the 4% of the business that will produce the big return on investment.

BALANCED SCORECARD

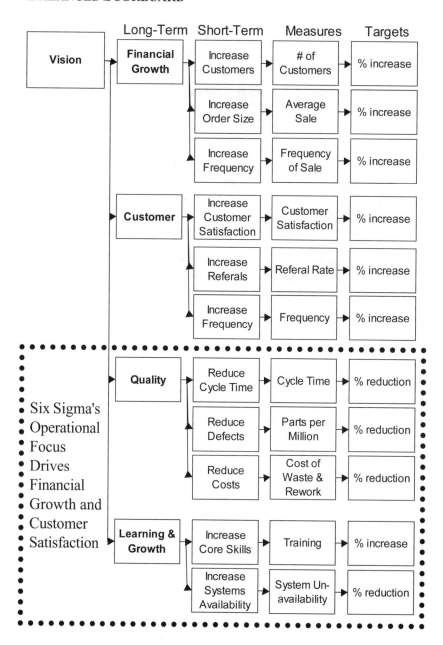

	Long-Term	Short-Term	Measures	Targets
Vision	**Financial Growth**	Increase Customers	# of Customers	% increase
		Increase Order Size	Average Sale	% increase
		Increase Frequency	Frequency of Sale	% increase
	Customer	Increase Customer Satisfaction	Customer Satisfaction	% increase
		Increase Referrals	Referal Rate	% increase
		Increase Frequency	Frequency	% increase
	Quality	Reduce Cycle Time	Cycle Time	% reduction
		Reduce Defects	Parts per Million	% reduction
		Reduce Costs	Cost of Waste & Rework	% reduction
	Learning & Growth	Increase Core Skills	Training	% increase
		Increase Systems Availability	System Un-availability	% reduction

Six Sigma's Operational Focus Drives Financial Growth and Customer Satisfaction

DOUBLE YOUR SPEED

How often have you or your customers wished that you could be faster at ordering, fulfilling, billing, or just answering the phone?

YOU CAN BE! Dynamic performance is not limited to a lucky few. There are known, specific methods and strategies for slashing cycle time without making anyone work any harder or faster. Find ways to reduce cycle time by 50-80-90% by:

1) defining the process,
2) identifying the root cause of delay, and
3) restructuring the process to eliminate the delay.

AD-HOC PROCESSES

Most processes, whether it's ordering, billing, manufacturing, or fulfilling an order, evolve from ad-hoc processes cobbled together at some earlier point in time. Over time, due to one calamity or another, they become more complex and convoluted. Departments are created to handle each step in the process. To "reduce costs," work is handled in increasingly large batches by specialized individuals. Each employee is busy working hard on their task, but their inbox stays full and their outbox just becomes someone else's inbox.

REDUCING CYCLE TIME

Whenever I work with a team of people about reducing cycle time, they all moan because they don't see how they can work any faster...and they're right. Speed is not about the people working harder or faster; it's about focusing on the customer's "lazy" order,

Here's the Secret: Your people are busy, but the "thing" going through the process is idle over 90% of the time. People are stunned to discover that in processes that take over 100 days, there may be less than one day of real work! In processes that seem to take eight hours, there may be less than 15 minutes of real work. All you have to do is find ways to remove the delay *between* process steps.

Using value-added analysis, you can slash cycle time by 50-80% or more.

CASE STUDY - MEDICAL CLAIMS

Last year I worked with a medical claims group. It was taking, on average, 140 days or more to process each claim. Upon examination, we found that processing the claim only consumed 7 hours (one day) of this time; the rest of the time the claim sat around waiting for something to happen. In just a two day session we found ways to shave almost 100 days off their cycle time. That's a 70% reduction in cycle time or a 3-fold increase in speed.

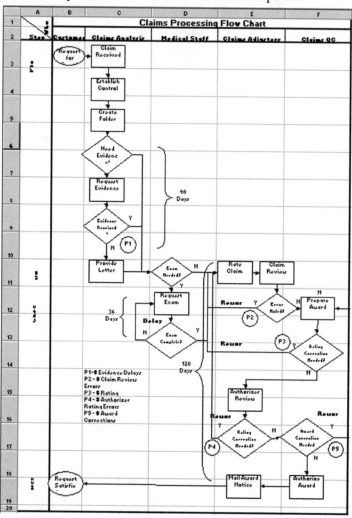

BREAK THE SPEED BARRIER!

Want to make breakthrough improvements in your speed? Here's how:

- **Flowchart your process** showing all of the activities (boxes), decisions (diamonds), and arrows connecting each box.

- Starting from the top of your flowchart, for each box, diamond, and arrow, **estimate the actual time it takes** to do that piece of the process. And don't buy the first answer you get. I asked the claims group how long it takes to receive and get a new claim into the queue. They said 25 days. Not true! It took about 10 minutes to log the form, 24 days before it got to a reviewer, and 45 minutes to validate the form. 55 minutes, not 25 days. For 24 days and 7 hours, the claim sat idle waiting for processing.

- **Now ask yourself, does this box, diamond, or arrow add value**? Value added things change, enhance, or improve the order. What's not value-added? Delay, idle time, inspection, rework, scrap, and so on.

- If a box, diamond, or arrow doesn't add value, **is there a way to reduce its impact or eliminate it** from the flow? In the claims example, there really was no reason for the claim to wait 24 days to be inspected. I recommended that they set a target to log and inspect a claim in less than 24 HOURS. We kept doing this with each major delay in the process to eliminate 100 days total.

- **Reduce inspection.** I wondered, do they have to inspect each incoming claim form? Using problem solving the team could identify the most common error in completing the form and redesign it to reduce or eliminate common errors. Then it wouldn't need to be inspected or it could be handled easily by a less experienced staff person.

- **Establish an action plan** to transition from the old, slow process to the newer, faster process. Start the new process using incoming orders and let existing orders drain out of the old process.

- **Find a way to "burn the bridges"** back to the old process. In one company, they removed the old individual workstations, which forced everyone to participate in learning to use the newer, higher speed ones.

- **Establish cycle time measures** to sustain the improvement, probably an XmR control chart for individual orders.

Want to make your customers happier? More loyal? Less likely to switch suppliers? In today's high-speed society, they want you to be faster, always faster. Using the simple tools of a flowchart and a value-added analysis, I've never failed to find 50-70 and even 90% reductions in cycle time. And you can too! It's a little grueling, pulling apart your process and nitpicking its flow, but you only have to do it once to discover the power in this process.

Double Your Quality

Purpose: Make Breakthrough Improvements in Speed, Quality, and Cost that save $250,000 or more per project.

Key Tools
- Line Graph (high-level focus)
- Pareto Chart (laser focus)
- Ishikawa (i.e., Fishbone) Diagram

Process

FISH	Step	Activity
Focus	1	Define the problem: Reduce delay, defects, or cost
	2	Analyze the problem
Improve	3	Implement the countermeasures
Sustain	4	Stabilize to lock in the improvements
Honor	5	Review, recognize, and refocus

LASER FOCUSED SWAT TEAMS

I often hear horror stories from companies that started lots of teams, let them choose their own problems to solve, and waited patiently for the money to start rolling in. Months pass; years pass. Teams become frustrated. "Six Sigma doesn't work!" they cry.

Don't let this happen to you!

LASER FOCUS EVERY TEAM YOU START.

This means that leadership will want to work with an improvement expert to develop the first two elements of a successful improvement story:

 Line graph showing defects (preferably in parts per million) over a period of time. (This answers the questions: "What's broken? How broken is it?")

 Pareto chart(s) showing 1, 2, or 3 "big bars" that contribute 50-60% of the problem identified in the line graph. Remember: 4% of any business creates over half of the waste and rework.

Developing the line and pareto charts should take no more than 3-5 days using existing data. Tip: download free tools for drawing these charts from www.qimacros.com/freestuff.html#downloads.

Tip: Never start by collecting new data. This is just a way of avoiding Six Sigma. And unless your business is completely ignorant of day-to-day operations and problems, you already have enough data to work with. Just get on with it.

Tip: Don't delegate. If a leader working with an improvement expert can't get to this level of specificity, neither can a team! Never start a team that doesn't have a good chance of success. You'll just waste their time and threaten the survival of Six Sigma.

IDENTIFY THE EXPERTS

Now that you've narrowed your focus, you can identify the experts who should be involved in the root cause analysis. This is another good reason to laser-focus your improvement efforts; otherwise you won't be able to get the right people on the team.

Mistakes Teams Make. In traditional improvement efforts, teams identify their own problems. Unfortunately, the team often chooses problems that aren't their's to solve. Often they focus on the pain caused by problems in their supplier's process, not their own. The problem they identify can't be solved by the existing team.

Or after the team develops the line and pareto charts, they discover that they no longer have the right people on the team to solve the problem.

Either way, laser-focusing the effort *before selecting a team* will save time and effort.

ANALYZE ROOT CAUSES

Once you get the experts in a room, conduct the root cause analysis in 4-8 hours. Traditional teams met once a week for an hour. This built weeks of delay into the process. If a problem's worth fixing, if it's a mission-critical problem, fix it fast! I've rarely had a team that couldn't find the root causes in a day or less. Then disband the root cause team and identify an implementation team (leaders and workers).

LASER FOCUS THE IMPLEMENTATION

Implementing the changes may take days, weeks or even months, depending on changes to information and other systems. Project manage the implementation and find another "big bar" and do another root cause analysis.

This approach will save you a fortune in time and money usually wasted on "shotgun" or "knee jerk" problem solving.

SIMPLE TOOLS

The good news is that you don't need a bunch of complex tools to go to 5 Sigma (0.03% defects or 300 defects per million). For the eyes, we invented telescopes to see into space and microscopes to see into the invisible. For companies, we invented a businesscope of quality tools. All you really need is a line graph, a pareto chart or two, and a fishbone diagram.

If you don't already have the QI Macros, you can get all of these charts in the QI Macros Demo: http://www.qimacros.com/QIDemo.exe. And you can download the user guide from http://www.qimacros.com/freestuff.html.

In a hospital, all you need is:

1. a line graph of infections per month or patient falls per month

2. a pareto chart identifying where most of these infections or falls occur (is it after surgery or in the patient's room? Is it a certain kind of patient?) This data is readily available in all hospitals.

3. Root cause analysis and a fishbone diagram to display the results.

In a computer operations environment, you might need:

1. a line graph of computer outages or application failures

2. a pareto chart or two of the "trouble tickets" reported for each system outage to narrow the focus to either the operating system, application software, computer hardware or network.

3. Root cause analysis and a fishbone diagram to display the results.

In a manufacturing environment, you might need:

1. a line graph of production defects

2. a pareto chart or two of the contributors to defects (materials, machines, methods, people or process.)

3. Root cause analysis and a fishbone diagram to display the results.

So think about your own environment. What data do you already have that will allow you to develop:

1. a line graph of the defect rate?

2. pareto charts of the various elements that contribute to these defects?

Draw these charts using Excel and the QI Macros, choose the most promising pareto chart (the one with a few big bars at the front and lots of little ones at the end). Schedule and conduct a series of half-day root cause analysis meetings with in-house experts on each of the "big bars" of the pareto chart.

Tip: Don't try to combine them; do each big bar separately. They often have different root causes.

Invariably, this results in finding and fixing some heretofore undetectable root causes and results in dramatic reductions in defect rates and the associated costs.

Using just these few tools, you can go from 3-to-5 sigma in 18-24 months. For more detail, download our FREE Money Belt Starter Kit: http://www.qimacros.com/freestuff.html.

CASE STUDY-COMPUTER OPERATIONS

One Baby Bell reduced computer downtime by 74% in just six months using Six Sigma.

DEFINE THE PROBLEM

At the beginning, there were 100,000 "seat" minutes of outage per week. Since there were 9,000 service representatives, that means only 11 minutes of outage per week per person, but all totalled, it meant the loss of 1667 hours, 208 person days, or five person weeks. In other words, it was the equivalent of having five more service reps available.

TARGET:

The VP of Operations set a goal of reducing this by 50% which caused a lot of grumbling, but on analysis, they found that 39% of the downtime was caused by the server software, 28% was caused by application software, and 27% server hardware.

ANALYZE THE PROBLEM

Multiple improvement teams tackled each of these areas. Root cause analysis and verification determined that password file corruption, faulty hardware boards, processes, and one application accounted for most of the failures.

PREVENT THE PROBLEM

Multiple countermeasures were implemented including up-grades to the operating system in over 600 servers to prevent password file corruption and other problems.

CHECK RESULTS

In less than six months they had exceeded the goal by achieving a 74% reduction in computer downtime.

SUSTAIN THE IMPROVEMENTS

A system was implemented to monitor and manage outages for both immediate and long-term improvement.

CASE STUDY-MAIL ORDER FULFILLMENT

In my business, I ship software and training materials. This results in a variety of possible fulfillment errors:

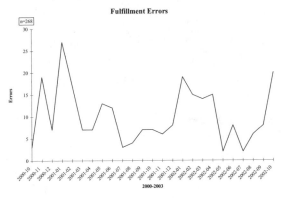

DEFINE THE PROBLEM

On average, we were getting 10 errors per month—about a 3% error rate. By analyzing each error, we were able to identify the most common types of errors;

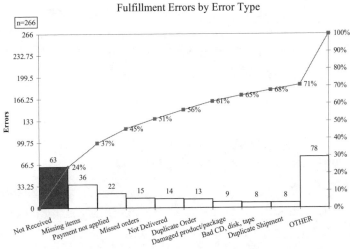

To analyze the problem that shipments were not being received, we then looked at the source of these errors by examining the invoices and any returned packages.

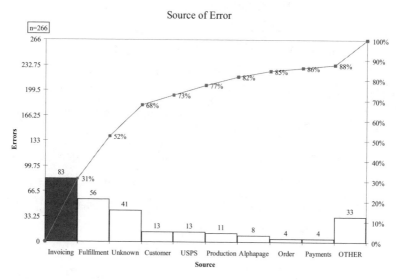

Source of Error

TARGET:

I set a goal of reducing these errors by 50%. As you can see from this chart, invoicing and fulfillment (packaging) contribute over 50% of the problem!

ANALYZE THE PROBLEM

Part of our problem involved the retyping of orders, resulting in address and order errors. Another involved tracking the shipped products.

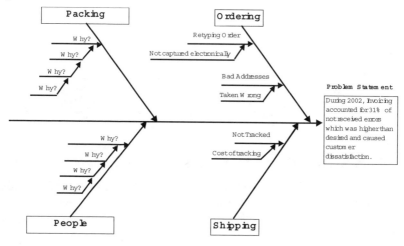

PREVENT THE PROBLEM

To prevent these problems we chose to:

1. Capture all internet orders electronically and import them into the billing software. Additionally, we decided to drive more customers to the website as opposed to the phone or fax.

2. Capture all phone orders electronically using the internet. (Type once and import.)

3. Use Stamps.com to create the shipping labels because:

   • Stamps.com validates the address using USPS data

   • Stamps.com provides FREE delivery confirmation ($0.45/ order savings).

CHECK RESULTS

It took about two months to implement all of these improvements. As a result, *total errors* have dropped from 10/month to 2.4/ month, a 75% reduction.

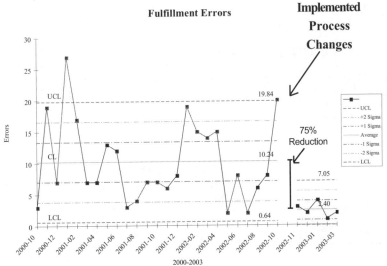

SUSTAIN THE IMPROVEMENTS

Using this data, we are now charting the errors per month using a c chart (above).

Six Sigma Tarpits

Recently, I facilitated a team that had been in existence for six months. All they had to show for their time was a flowchart of a process that was mainly rework. I'd been calling every few days for weeks nagging the team for data about how the process performs. I got part of the data the night before the meeting and the rest of the data by lunch. But after a morning of trying to sort through the issues surrounding the process, the team had fallen into "storming" about the whole process. They were frustrated and so was I.

Pitfall #1: Starting a team when you have no data (line graph and pareto chart minimum) that indicates you have a problem that can be solved using Six Sigma. Without data to guide you, you don't know who should be on the team, so you end up with different groups trying to solve different problems.

Solution: Set the team up for success. 1) Work with data you already have; don't start a team to collect a bunch of new data. 2) Refine your problem before you let a group of people get in a room to analyze root causes. You can guarantee a team's success by laser focusing the problem to be solved.

Pitfall #2: Questionable data. To throw a team off its tracks, some member who doesn't like the implications of the data will state in a congruent voice that the data is clearly wrong. If you let it, this will derail the team into further data analysis. I know from experience that all data is imperfect. It has been systematically distorted to make the key players look good and manipulate the reward system, but it is the "systematic" distortion that allows you to use the data anyway.

Solution: Recognize that this member is operating on gut feel, not data. Simply ask: "Okay, do you have better data? (They don't.) Then how do you know the data's invalid? (I just know.) How do you know? (Instinct, gut feel.) Well, unless you have better data that proves this is invalid, we're going to continue using this data. You're welcome to go get your data, but meanwhile, we're moving forward." If the person is unwilling to continue, you can excuse them from the team because they will continue to sabotage the progress.

Pitfall #3: Whalebone diagrams. When searching for root causes, if your fishbone diagram turns into a "whalebone" diagram that covers several walls, then your original problem statement was too big.

Solution: Go back to your pareto chart. Take the biggest bar down a level to get more specific. Then go back to root cause analysis.

Pitfall #4: Boiling the ocean. Teams have an unflinching urge to fix big problems. If you've done a good job of laser focusing your problem, you'll have a specific type of defect in a specific area to focus on. If you let the team expand its focus, you'll end up whalebone diagramming and have to go back to a specific problem.

Solution: Get the team to agree to solve just this one issue, because its solution will probably improve several other elements of the overall problem. Assure them that you'll come back to the other pieces of the problem, but first you have to nail this one down.

Sustain The Improvement

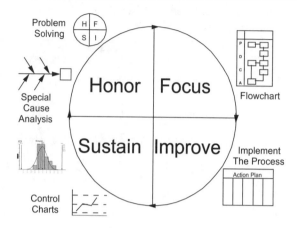

Purpose: Sustain and Monitor the Improvement

Key Tools
- Flow Chart
- Control Chart (stability)
- Histogram (capability)

Process

FISH Step		Activity
Focus	1	Refine the process
	2	Identify the "quality" and "process" indicators
Improve	3	Implement the process and quality indicators
Sustain	4	Check the process for stability and capability
Honor	5	Review, recognize, and refocus Continue Improvement

DEFINE THE PROCESS

Define the improved process as a starting point.

A flowchart uses a few simple symbols to show the flow of a process. The symbols are:

⬭	Start/End	Customer initiated
▢	Activity	Adding value (verb–noun)
◇	Decision	Choosing among two or more alternatives
→	Arrow	Showing the flow and transition
○	Indicator	Measurement (defects, time, cost)

Instead of writing directly on the flowchart, use small Post-it™ notes for both the decisions and activities. This way, the process will remain easy to change until you have it clearly and totally defined. Limit the number of decisions and activities per page. Move detailed subprocesses onto additional pages.

Across the **top** of the flowchart list every person or department that helps deliver the product or service. Along the **left-hand side**, list the major steps in your process: planning, doing, checking, and acting to improve. Even going to the grocery store involves creating a list (plan), getting the groceries (do), checking the list, and acting to get any forgotten item.

Hint: You can draw these in Microsoft Excel using the drawing toolbar. Click on View-Toolsbars-Drawing and then click on autoshapes.

YARDSTICKS AND MICROMETERS

The measurements of customer requirements usually occur after the end product or service is delivered. To ensure that customers get what they want, you will want to set up a system of early warning indicators that will predict whether or not the process will deliver what the customers want. Like the quality indicators, these predictive indicators will need to measure defects, time, and cost *inside the process*.

EASIEST POINTS TO MEASURE:

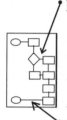

- **process indicators** are at the *key handoffs* (to measure time or missed commitments) or *decision points* (to measure defects and rework). If, for example, you were trying to *predict* how long it would take to get to work, the number of red lights or average highway speed could *predict* your total commute time.

- **quality indicators** (e.g., total commute time) *after* the product or service has been delivered. Looking back at the main flowchart, at what points could you most easily take measurements that would predict whether the process will be able to deliver what the customers want?

"Quality" Requirements Indicator	"Process" Early Warning Indicator
Percent defective	Amount of rework per step Number of defects per step
Missed Commitments	Time per process step Delay (idle, rework time)
Value	Cost of waste and rework
Paycheck errors	Timesheet errors % timesheets late
Appliance installation time	Old appliance removal time
Cost of food spoilage	Number of customers Perishable food ordered

PULSE MONITORS TO PREDICT PERFORMANCE

A stable process produces PREDICTABLE RESULTS CONSISTENTLY. Process stability can be easily determined using control charts. A control chart is a line graph of your data (the same line graph used to identify and focus your problem) with average and sigma lines to determine stability. The average and sigma lines (+- 1, 2 and 3 sigma) are calculated from the data. The Upper Control Limit (UCL) is the +3 sigma line and the Lower Control Limit (LCL) is the -3 sigma line. 99.7% of all data points should fall between these two limits. See: qimacros.com/qiwizard/sustain.html

COMMON AND SPECIAL CAUSES OF VARIATION

How can you tell if a process is stable? Processes are never perfect. Common and special causes of variation make the process perform differently in different situations. **Common Cause:** Getting from your home to school or work takes varying amounts of time because of traffic or transportation delays. These are common causes of variation; they exist every day. **Special Cause:** A blizzard, a traffic accident, a chemical spill or other freak occurrence would be a special cause of variation. Processes that are "out of control" need to be stabilized before they can be improved. Special causes, require immediate cause-effect analysis to eliminate the special cause of variation. The QI Macros for Excel calculates unstable points or trends for you.

AVOID THE PITFALLS

Pitfall #1: Confusing Control Limits and Specification Limits. Many people confuse control limits, which are calculated based on your data with specification limits that are provided by your customers.

Solution: You can add specification limits to a control chart as a "target" or "goal" line.

Pitfall #2: Getting caught up in formulas and statistics behind the charts and forgetting to interpret the results.

Solution: Use an SPC software package like the QI Macros for Excel and free yourself up to analyze the results and improve the process.

CHOOSING THE RIGHT CONTROL CHART

Do you need to monitor how long it takes to deliver a product or service, the number of defects per product, or the cost of waste or rework?

Time, cost, length, and weight are known as *variable* data.

Counting the number of defects or defective items gives *attribute* or *counted* data.

The type of data (attribute or variable) and the size of the sample taken (1, 2-10, or total) will determine the type of graph used to measure the process.

Regardless of sample size, each of these charts can be drawn easily as a *control chart*. **Tip:** If the math seems scary, get the QI Macros for Microsoft® Excel to automate your charts.

• The **X axis** (horizontal) shows how often the data is collected (daily, hourly, weekly, periodically).

• The **Y axis** (vertical) shows:

- the number or percent defective (c, np, p, u)

- the time, cost, length, weight, etc. (XR charts)

Then, based on the type of data and sample size, the software will calculate the upper and lower control limits (UCL, LCL) and center line (CL) that will make it possible to evaluate process stability.

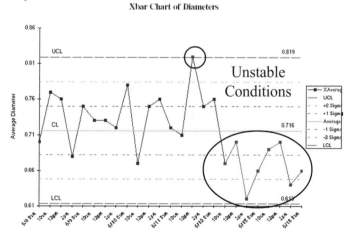

Xbar Chart of Diameters

CHOOSING THE RIGHT CONTROL CHART

One area that most people seem to struggle with is choosing the right control chart. The right chart is based on the type of data, attribute (counted) or variable (measured), and the sample size.

FOR ATTRIBUTE DATA USE NP, P, C AND U CHARTS

If you are counting defective items (e.g incorrect orders)

- use a np chart if the sample size is constant

- use a p chart if the sample size varies

If you are counting the # of defects on each item
    (e.g. number of errors on an order)

- use a c chart if the sample size is constant or very large

- use a u chart if the sample size varies

FOR VARIABLE DATA USE XmR, XbarR, AND XbarS

- if the sample size is one use an XmR chart
- if the sample size is 2-10 use an XbarR chart
- if the sample size is 11-25 use an XbarS chart

To watch a control chart with stability analysis being built by the QI Macros go to http://www.qimacros.com/cchart.rm

Choosing The Right Chart

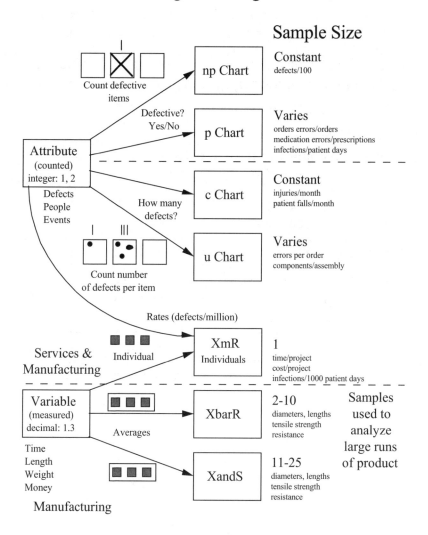

ARE YOUR PROCESSES PREDICTABLE?

Processes that are "out of control" need to be stabilized before they can be improved using the problem-solving process. Special causes require immediate cause-effect analysis to eliminate the variation.

The following diagram will help you evaluate stability and predictability of any control chart. Unstable conditions can be any of the following:

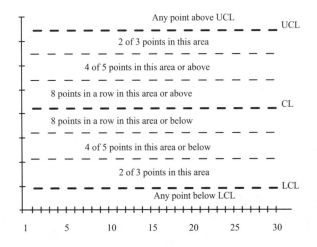

Any of these conditions suggests an unstable condition may exist. Consider investigating the special cause of variation.

Use the Ishikawa diagram to analyze potential root causes.

Once you've eliminated the special causes, you can turn your attention to using the problem solving process to reduce the common causes of variation:

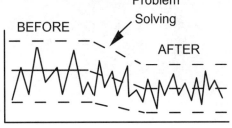

GOAL POSTS TO ANALYZE PROCESS CAPABILITY

A capable process MEETS THE CUSTOMER'S REQUIRE-
MENTS 100% OF THE TIME. The Upper (USL) and Lower
(LSL) Specification Limits are determined from the customer's
requirements.

Attribute Capability: The capability of counted (i.e. attribute)
data like defects is zero defects. Customers hate defects, outages, etc.

Variable Capability: The capability of measured (i.e. variable)
data like time, money, age, length, weight, etc. is determined using
the customer's specifications and a histogram. When a customer
defines an upper and a lower specification limit for a product or
service, whether it's the diameter of a shaft or the time in line at a fast
food restaurant, all points within the two limits are considered
"good." The process capability index (Cp) indicates how well the
data fits between the USL and the LSL. Cpk on the other hand
indicates how centered the data is within the range. If both Cp and
Cpk are greater than or equal to 1 then the process is considered
capable. Cp and Cpk of 1.0 is equivalent to 3 sigma. 1.33 is 4 Sigma.
1.67 is 5 Sigma. 2.0 is 6 sigma.

To automate these charts, consider using the QI Macros.

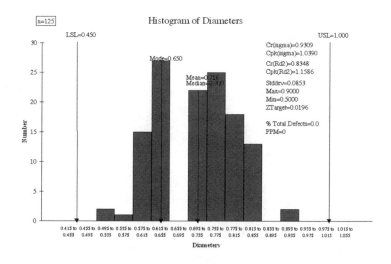

ANALYZING PROCESS CAPABILITY

When Cp, the process capability index, and Cpk, the centering index, are over 1.0, the process is capable, but most manufacturers require Cp>1.33 (4 sigma).

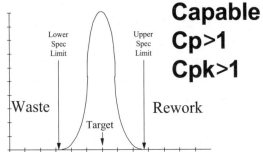

Use the problem solving process to identify and prevent the root causes of waste (usually below the lower specification limit) and rework (usually above the upper specification limit). The goal, is to reduce variation so that all of your points fit within the specification limits, clustered around a target.

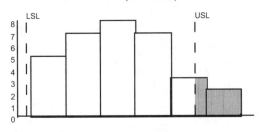

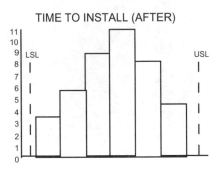

Designing a Purple Cow

Process improvements are a key part of Six Sigma, but so is designing new products or services. In Seth Godin's recent book, *Purple Cow*, he suggests that every company should be focused on remarkable products that a small "hive" of determined sneezers will seek out. Products so remarkable that they sell themselves.

Unknowingly, when I created the QI Macros, I created a Purple Cow—a product so easy to use and already integrated with Microsoft Excel that everyone from hospital quality managers to Fortune 50 Blackbelts have been leaping on board. In the process, they've been abandoning their expensive, complex statistical software for the ease of the QI Macros. Over half of all my sales come from word of mouth referrals.

As I have continued to evolve the QI Macros, I've used Quality Function Deployment (QFD) as my guide to thinking through the design and development of new functionality. It doesn't matter how small or large your product or service, QFD can help you design a purple cow in less time with higher quality.

Wouldn't it be great to hit the ground running with a Six Sigma capable (3.4 defects per million) process for delivering your product or service? Of course it would, but most 3-Sigma companies don't have the stomach for the kind of rigorous thinking it takes to design and launch a new product or service at these levels. Unless, of course, you understand the horrendous costs associated with a typical "seat of the pants" implementation.

Design for Six Sigma requires the application of three key tools: QFD, FMEA, and DOE.

QFD—Quality Function Deployment-is a rigorous method for translating customer needs, wants, and wishes into step-by-step procedures for delivering the product or service. While delivering better designs tailored to customer needs, QFD also cuts the normal development cycle by 50%, making you faster to market.

Failure Modes and Effects Analysis helps anticipate problems.

Design of Experiments identifies optimal ways to do things.

BETTER DESIGNS IN HALF THE TIME

QFD uses the "QFD House of Quality" (a template in the QI Macros) to help structure your thinking, making sure nothing is left out. There are four key steps to QFD thinking:

1. Product Planning- Translating what the customer wants (in their language, e.g., portable, convenient phone service) into a list of prioritized product/service design requirements (in your language, e.g., cell phones) that describe how the product works. It also compares your performance with your competition's, and sets targets for improvement to differentiate your product/service from your competitor's.

2. Part Planning - Translating product specifications (design criteria from step 1) into part characteristics (e.g., light weight, belt-clip, battery-driven, not-hardwired but radio-frequency based).

3. Process Planning - Translating part characteristics (from step 2) into optimal process characteristics that maximize your ability to deliver Six Sigma quality (e.g., ability to "hand off" a cellular call from one antenna to another without interruption).

4. Production Planning - Translating process characteristics (from step 3) into manufacturing or service delivery methods that will optimize your ability to deliver Six Sigma quality in the most efficient manner (e.g., cellular antennas installed with overlapping coverage to eliminate dropped calls).

Even in my small business, I often use this template to evaluate and design a new product or service. It helps me think through every aspect of what my customers want and how to deliver it. It saves me a lot of "clean up" on the backend. It doesn't always mean that I get everything right, but I get more of it right, which translates into greater sales and higher profitability with less rework on my part.

That's the power of QFD.

Risk-Free Formula For Six Sigma Success

Over half of all Six Sigma implementations seem to be failing. In the language of Six Sigma, that's 1-2 Sigma…a pathetic track record. And if you study how most companies are implementing Six Sigma, you'll find **the same old formula that ruined TQM**:

1. Get top leadership to commit to widespread implementation.
2. Train internal trainers (Black Belts) to minimize the costs of training everyone else.
3. Internal trainers train team leaders (Green Belts)
4. Start a bunch of teams
5. Hope for the best.

Everyone points to GE as a leader in Six Sigma, but if you look more closely you'll see that Jack Welch had already created a company that managed and even embraced change. So implementing Six Sigma wasn't as hard as it might be in other organizations.

Many people I talk to in various industries say that they tried process improvement and it left a bad taste in their mouths. So Six Sigma not only has to overcome resistance to change, but also the bad taste left by failed TQM implementations.

Remember the Secrets

So how do you implement Six Sigma in a way that's risk free?

1. Leverage the network of informal leaders, not the hierarchical structure of formal leaders
2. Set BHAGS (50% reductions in defects and delay)
3. To boost returns, *narrow your focus* (4-50 rule)
4. Small changes will have big effects (4-50 rule)
5. To increase adoption, *reduce* the number of people involved
6. An ounce of experience is worth a pound of training (use just-in-time training before problem solving).
7. Start at the headwaters of your river of defects and delay, not the mouth (e.g., call centers).

ENCOURAGE ADOPTION

By using the proven power of diffusion. Diffusion research suggests a much safer route to successful implementation of Six Sigma or any change.

The employee body can make three choices about Six Sigma or any change: adopt, adapt, or reject. In a world of too much to do and too little time, rejection is often the first impulse. People rarely adopt methods completely, so there must be room for adaptation to fit the corporate environment. There are five factors that affect the speed and success of Six Sigma adoption:

1. Trialability-How easy is it to "test drive" Six Sigma?
2. Simplicity-How difficult is it to understand? (Simplify!)
3. Relative benefit-What does it offer over and above what I'm already doing? (How is it better than trial-and-error?)
4. Compatibility-How well does it match our environment?
5. Observability-How easy is it for leaders and opinion makers (sneezers) to see the benefit?

You can also speed up adoption by letting the employees decide for themselves to adopt Six Sigma rather than having the CEO decide for them (although this is how we keep preaching success-get the CEO to commit to widespread change). So, to maximize your chance of success and minimize your initial investment:

1. Start small. Use the 4-50 rule. Less than 4% of any business creates over half the waste and rework. So you don't have to involve more than 4% of your employees or spend a lot of money on widespread training to get results. Get an external Six Sigma consultant to help you find and create solutions using the tools and methods of Six Sigma. Your employees will learn through experience which is far more valuable than classroom training.

2. Set BHAGs (Big Hairy Audacious Goals). Go for 50% reduction in cycle time, defects, or costs. When you're just starting out, big reductions are often easier to get than you might think, so why not go for them? This also telegraphs the message to your teams that this ain't continuous improvement.

3. Fly under the radar. Most companies broadcast their Six Sigma initiative, and employees think: "Here comes another one." This usually stirs up the laggards and skeptics-what I call the corporate "immune system." You are much better off to make initial teams successful and let the "word of mouth" spread through informal networks, because this is the fastest way for cultures to adopt change.

4. Create initial success. In 1980, the company I worked for brought in a trial of 20 TSO terminals (to replace the punched cards IT used). They selected a small group of programmers to use the terminals. The buzz from this one group caused TSO to be immediately accepted and integrated into the workforce. Do the same thing for Six Sigma. Only start teams that can succeed. Make a small group of early adopters successful. Then another, then another.

When the pioneers (early adopters) become successful, they will tell their friends. The pioneers will convince the early settlers who will eventually convince the late settlers. No one will ever convince the laggards and skeptics; they have to convince themselves.

5. Fight the urge to widen your focus; remember the dark side of the 80/20 rule: 80% of your effort will only produce 20% of the benefit.

6. Simplify. Using simple tools like line graphs, pareto charts, and fishbone diagrams, you can easily move from 3 to 5 Sigma (300 parts per million) in 18-24 months. There are more complex tools like QFD and DOE in Six Sigma, but you won't be ready to Design For Six Sigma (DFSS) until you simplify and streamline your existing processes and lay the groundwork for it.

7. Review and refocus. Once you solve the initial 4% of your core problems, start on the next 4%, then the next. Diffusion research has shown that somewhere between 16-25% involvement will create a "critical mass" that will cause the change to sweep through the culture.

GOOD NEWS ABOUT PRODUCTIVITY AND PROFITABILITY

When you focus on the 4% that creates over half the waste and rework, your initial teams get big benefits: 50% reduction in defects, waste, and rework and $250,000/project improvement in the bottom line. By the time you've worked your way through the first 16-20% of your problems, you will get 80% (the 80/20 rule) of the benefits of Six Sigma. And you'll have minimized your costs of implementation. Now you can grow skilled internal Black Belts from your initial improvement team members. And you can begin to think about DFSS to design your processes to deliver Six Sigma quality.

Six Sigma payoffs are huge, but you may want to consider using the power of diffusion to ensure that the methods and tools take root in your business and flourish. But it's up to you. You can choose the conventional wisdom which gives you only a 50-50 chance at success or choose the power of diffusion which increases your odds substantially.

JUMP START YOUR SUCCESS

We offer telephone and email coaching to help you make sure your initial teams will succeed. We also offer on-site "resulting" to help you laser-focus and solve your first few mission-critical problems. We can help you "learn to swim" without the fear of drowning in your own data or Six Sigma methods and tools.

Call now: 888-468-1537

or visit our website at: **www.qimacros.com.**

Jay Arthur, The KnowWare® Man, works with operational managers who want to systematically cut costs and boost profits. Using Jay's approach, one Baby Bell eliminated five of their top order errors in just four months, resulting in monthly savings of $250,000. Haven't you waited long enough to start using a proven method for routinely saving $250,000 or more and adding it back into your bottom line?

Six Sigma Simplified

Step 1 - Focus

Factory
Fix-it: **Defects + Delay = Cost**
Main: **Quality + Speed = Profit**

Tools

Tree Diagram

Line Graph

Pareto Chart
4-50 Rule

Cost of Quality

Step 2 - Improve

Quality   Speed

Root Cause Analysis	Value Analysis
(Why, Why, Why?)	(Where?)
	Hint: It's the Arrows

Tools

Fishbone (Ishikawa)   Flow Chart

Countermeasures   Value-Added
Verify Root Causes   Worksheet
Line Graph
Pareto Chart

F I
H S

Step 4 - Honor

Recognize, Review, Refocus

What did we do right?

Where else can we apply
what we've learned?

What's next?

Step 3 - Sustain

Monitor and Sustain
New Levels of Performance in
Mission Critical Systems

Tools

Flow Chart

Control Charts
(Stability)

Histogram
(Capability)

Key Tools

 Tree Diagram: Systematically link ideas, targets, objectives, goals, or activities in greater and greater detail. It shows key goals, sub goals, measures, and tasks required to accomplish an objective.

 Matrix: Compare two or more groups of ideas, determine relationships among the elements, and make decisions. It helps prioritize tasks or issues to aid decision making and shows linkages between large groups of characteristics, functions, and tasks.

 Line Graph: Show data trends over time. The Y-axis (left) shows the defects, time, cost and the X-axis (bottom) shows time (minute, hour, day, week, etc.).

 Pareto Chart: Focus the improvement effort by identifying the 20% (vital few) of the contributors that create 80% of the time delay, defects, or costs in any process.

 Cause-Effect: Systematically analyze the root causes of problems It begins with major causes and works backward to root causes.

 Flowchart: Show the flow of work through a process including all activities, decisions, and measurement points.

 Control Chart: Help analyze, sustain, and monitor the current levels of process *stability* and to identify key issues for problem solving or root cause analysis.

 Histogram: Determine the *capability* (i.e., the level of performance the customers can consistently expect) of the process and the distribution of measurable data.

FREE DOWNLOADS AVAILABLE FROM

www.qimacros.com/freestuff.html

- Problem Solving Software (Line, Pareto, Ishikawa in Self-Installing Format (250kb)
  Download Free Macintosh version (Click Here).

- QI Macros User Guide (1Mb PDF)

- Articles on using Excel for SPC, ISO, and Six Sigma Control Chart Formulas and Stability Analysis

- Six Sigma Money Belt Action Plan

- Six Sigma Quick Reference Card

- SPC Quick Reference Card

YES! I WANT JAY ARTHUR'S FAST, FUN AND EASY-TO-USE SIX SIGMA SYSTEM TO WORK FOR ME!

PLEASE SEND THE SOFTWARE, TRAINING MATERIAL, AUDIO AND VIDEO INDICATED BELOW.

❏ Complete 6σ System Item# 290	❏ QI Macros for Excel Item# 230
QI Macros for Excel Software (#230)	QI Macros For Excel Software
QI Macros Training CD-ROM #(237)	3.5 inch floppy disk and
Six Sigma Tools Example Book (#239)	36 page User Guide
192 pg. Instructor Guide (#210)	**Only $137**
128 pg. Six Sigma Simplified (#205)	*includes $8 U.S. S&H*
180 min. Video & 240 min. Audio	*Add $20 for FedEx*
60 min. SPC Simplified Video	*Prices good until 12/31/03*
Only $495.95 Save $90	
Add $15 U.S. S&H , Add $35 for Fed Ex	

Please type or print clearly or attach business card here

Your Name _____

Company _____

Mailing Address _____

P.O. Box _____ Apt/Ste. _____

City, ST, Zip _____

Phone _____

Fax _____

Email _____

Purchase Order Number _____

❏ VISA ❏ MasterCard ❏ AMEX

_____Exp._____

Signature _____

Order and download software on-line at **www.qimacros.com**

Toll-Free Fax: **(888)468-1536** or (303) 753-9675

Mail: LifeStar, 2244 S. Olive St.
                   Denver, CO 80224-2518

Orders-only, Toll-free: (888) 468-1535 or (303) 757-2039

Questions: 888-468-1537 or 303-756-9144